The Jesus Prayer
An Orthodox Tradition

John W. Larson

Cover photo of Agia Sofia (St. Sophia's Church) in the village of Monemvasia, Greece, taken by Vicky Paraschou

ISBN-13: 9781499385892
ISBN-10: 1499385897
Library of Congress Control Number: 2014908852
CreateSpace Independent Publishing Platform
North Charleston, South Carolina

John Larson's permit to visit Mount Athos, Greece, in 1965

This book is dedicated to Father Parry, the beloved priest at Saint George Greek Orthodox Church in Saint Paul, Minnesota, from 1975 to 1999.

CONTENTS

PREFACE

After the 17th century and well into our own, English-speaking individuals not equipped with Greek, Russian, or at least French had to be content with secondhand information concerning Eastern spirituality. Steven Runciman in *The Great Church in Captivity* explains, "With the coming of the eighteenth century the West lost interest in the Orthodox faith, except to denounce it as obscurantist and debased. Even the Roman missionary effort was reduced" (319).

For the West, the Eastern Church was out of turn with the rationalism of the enlightened 18th century and Western enthusiasm for the Greek national uprising against the Turks in the early 19th century was not inspired by Byzantine Christianity but by the Golden Age of an ancient

Greece of their imagination. For them the greatest contribution of the Eastern Church had been the preservation of manuscripts of that Golden Age. Two examples illustrate prevailing 19th century attitudes toward the Eastern Church.

The first is that of Samuel Irenaeus Prime, a Presbyterian and editor of *The New York Observer*. Prime passed through Athens in the early 1850s as part of a yearlong tour of Europe and the Eastern Mediterranean. In Athens, not unlike a modern day tourist, he spent most of his time searching out and admiring Greek antiquities. But one Sunday toward the end of his stay, he attended church at Saint Irene's. There was a special service in honor of "some dead saint."

The language of the sermon was "so different from the ancient Greek as we pronounce it" that Prime was only able to catch a word here and there. So he looked about at the "pictures." Some were rather well done, he thought, but many were "of saints, male and female, to whom I had no introduction." The worst part came after the sermon.

"A doleful wail was set up by a few men near the altar, or where the altar would be in a Roman church; probably it was meant to be singing." This was continued until it became "intolerable." Equally distasteful, a company of gorgeously robed priests, in a room partitioned from the church and which might, he thought, be the Holy of holies, now marched around a table, bearing lighted candles, and bowing as they passed before an image of the Savior crucified." This went on until Prime and his party were "sick and tired of seeing it" and they left.

Later in the day they visited the home of the missionary Dr. Jonas King, who, at a time when Greece did not yet know religious tolerations, prudently held chapel in his own home. There the company, including many Greeks, behaved with "decorum and solemnity" and Prime was deeply impressed. "To be in Athens is an event in any man's life; but to hear Jonas King preaching the Gospel at the foot of Mars's hill is a joy to be cherished in memory even in heaven" (Prime, Vol. II, p. 215).

Prime's confident expression of disdain for the Eastern Church suggests he fully anticipated sympathy for his point of view from his mid-19th century American readers. But the same disdain openly expressed went on in the Anglo-Saxon world throughout the rest of the century.

In the 11th edition of the Encyclopedia Britannica, first published in 1910, and which enjoys the respect of scholars even to this day, one finds more balanced treatment of the theological questions dividing the Eastern and Western Churches, although aspects of the Eastern Church, monasticism in particular, are patently false.

Monks on Mount Athos, an article on Orthodoxy explains, are "for the most part ignorant and unlettered" (Vol. 20, p. 236). They share with the Turks responsibility for destroying many of the priceless classical manuscripts once housed in their libraries. The Turks used parchments to make cartridges during the Greek War of Independence, while the "neglect and vandalism" of the monks, who "it is said used the material as bait in fishing" finished off many more (Vol. II, p. 852).

There is no suggestion in the 1910 Encyclopedia that the monks practiced any particular form of spirituality. An entry on the "Hesychasts" discusses the controversy between Gregory Palamas (1296-1359) and Barlaam the Calabrian. Referring to Hesychast practices as "obviously related to certain well-known forms of Oriental mysticism," the chief significance attributed to the mid-fourteenth century debate is that the victory of Hesychasm was for the Greeks "an additional ground for separation from the Roman church" (Vol. 13, p. 414).

That a Hesychast tradition survived on Mount Athos and elsewhere in the Orthodox world was either unknown or considered insignificant. This was to change as the 20th century progressed and Orthodoxy, for various reasons, became better understood in the West.

APPENDIX

The author, John W. Larson, explains that this study was prepared in connection with History 5970 in the Modern Greek Studies Program at the University of Minnesota, under the direction of Professor Theo Stavrou. The lectures were carried out by James W. Cunningham, a professor of history at the College of St. Catherine in St. Paul during the fall semester of 1986. Dr. Cunningham found the paper inspiring and recommended it for publication.

I

THE EARLY 20TH CENTURY

In Rome, Pope Benedict XV (1914-1922) was inclined to be friendly toward the Orthodox churches, especially those recognizing the Papacy but practicing Eastern rites. Increasingly during Benedict's pontificate one might experience the liturgy of the Eastern rites celebrated in one of the Roman churches. Benedict seemed aware that new ease of communication was bringing the material world closer together and sensed the need for a corresponding drawing together of the spiritual world (Jon, Eric, editor, *The Pope: A Concise Biographical History*, New York: 1964, Vol. II, p. 463).

Elsewhere in the West, the "classical-rational" tradition, as Oxford-educated Robert

Byron called it, saw little of value in post-classical Eastern culture. The traditional view, taken from Edward Gibbon, regarded the Byzantine Empire as decadent and unworthy. Byron attacked this view with aggressive enthusiasm in his own history of the empire, published in 1929, when the author was barely twenty-four years old.

Byron's *The Byzantine Achievement* was an elaborate history of the empire, contentious even in its bibliography. There, speaking of the history of the Orthodox Church, he cautions, "Those wishing to study this subject and its particular aspects are warned against the numerous works of the English Roman and Anglo-Catholics. Under cover of spurious erudition and pretended impartiality, they exhibit a feminine spite, which makes the reader realize, after hours of attention, that he has been wasting his time" (quoted in Fussel, p.88).

But Robert Byron's contentious book is perhaps less well remembered today than works by his contemporary from Cambridge University, Steven Runciman, who, with the publication of *Byzantine Civilization* in 1933, began a lifetime of Byzantine studies, many of which are still in print. Byron and Runciman are but two examples of English scholarly interest in Byzantium, which began to take hold in the late 1920s and blossomed in the 1930s. A companion of Byron's, David Talbot Rice, who traveled to Mount Athos with Byron in 1927, subsequently became an art historian devoting much of his energy to the study of icons. His *Byzantine Art* was published in 1935.

Significantly, these young British authors of the 20s and 30s, with their enthusiastic interest in the Christian East rather than traditional Classical studies, were mainstream Protestant Anglo-Saxons. But unlike Mr. Prime a hundred years earlier, they sensed the Christian East had something to offer. Byron, a distant relative, incidentally, of the poet Lord Byron, came close to describing just what it was he found appealing.

Byron was twenty-two when he first visited Mount Athos in 1926. He went again the following year and in 1928 published a book about his experiences there, *The Station*. Not a pious book, nevertheless in *The Station* Byron treats the monks with sympathy, and more importantly, contrasts post World War I life

in England, which he finds aimless and inco-
herent, "a world of arid sequences," with the
intensity and "purity of focus" which he per-
ceived as dominating life on Athos. The search
for meaning and for "purity of focus" may
explain why some of Byron's generation, not
only in England but elsewhere in Europe, were
drawn to the Christian East

II

ORTHODOXY COMES WEST

The 1920s saw other developments that added to Western understanding of Orthodoxy. One was the revolution in Russia after which one million Russians, many priests and several Bishops, sought homes elsewhere, mostly in the West. Centers of Russian Orthodoxy were established at Munich and Paris. In Paris, the Institute of Saint Sergius, founded in 1925, became an important point of contact between Orthodox and Unorthodox. During the 1920s, an unusually brilliant group of scholars gathered at Saint Sergius and eventually three of them, Fathers Georges Florovsky, Alexander Schmemann, and John Meyendorff came to the United States.

The Saint Sergius group of teachers was prolific, publishing some seventy books and numerous articles between 1925 and 1944. The works of Schmemann and Meyendorff, now translated into English, have found wide, if not popular, acceptance in this country and England (Ware, p. 186). But in the 1920s it was not so much the works of these theologians which brought the West in touch with Orthodox spirituality as the translation into Western languages of an anonymous popular Russian story, *The Way of a Pilgrim* and its sequel, *The Pilgrim Continues His Way*.

III

THE WAY OF A PILGRIM

The Way of a Pilgrim was first published in the West in Berlin in 1926 in a German translation. A French edition was published in 1928, and in 1930 two different English translations appeared in London. Translated into Western languages at a time when many suffered bitter disillusionment brought on by the First World War and hungered for spiritual nourishment, *The Way of a Pilgrim* all but popularized an aspect of Orthodox spirituality hitherto little known in the West, the Jesus Prayer.

A synopsis of *The Way of the Pilgrim* was published in 1926. It read in part:

A Russian peasant who was literate but handicapped with a crippled left arm was seized with an ardent desire for continual prayer. Failing to learn the secret of it from sermons, he finally met the director he needed, a starets. The starets taught him to say the Jesus Prayer 3,000 times a day to begin with, then 6,000 times, then 12,000 times, than as often as he wished. In the end it was no longer the pilgrim saying a prayer but the prayer saying itself in the pilgrim's mind and heart whatever his occupation and even while he slept. The effects were marvelous: "in my soul I felt the bliss of loving God, interior peace, ecstasy, purity of thoughts, and a blessed awareness of God." (Quoted by Hausherr, pp. iii, iv)

The summary is inadequate, for it conveys none of the variety and charm of the pictures of Russian life that the Pilgrim encounters as he wanders in search of his quest from one place to another, and it neglects to tell of the *Philokalia*, the book which accompanies the Pilgrim on his wanderings. Still it reveals a number of things which are important. The Pilgrim, a layman, neither a priest nor a monk, was not able to find the answers to his spiritual quest at services in the churches he visited. He had to find a spiritual father, or starets, to teach him the prayer and guide him in its use. The prayer is clearly short and meant to be repeated frequently, even while engaged in other occupations. The result of mastering continuous use of the prayer was inward peace and communion with God.

IV

FRANNY AND ZOOEY

Anticipation of inward peace and communion with God doubtless tempted readers of *The Way of the Pilgrim* to proceed with the Jesus Prayer on their own, without a starets. Such is the situation described in the popular novel by J. D. Salinger, *Franny and Zooey*, which first appeared in *The New Yorker* in two parts in January 1955 and May 1957, appeared as a book in September 1961, and had such appeal that it was reprinted a dozen times in the twelve months following.

It is the 20-year-old Franny, college student and aspiring actress, who in Salinger's novel has read *The Way of the Pilgrim* and is obviously experimenting with its practice when she meets her boyfriend at his Ivy League college town for a weekend date. Shortly after arriving, she, distressed, pale, and with little beads of sweat on her brow, tells him the story of the Russian pilgrim, a "holy book," the "Philokalia," and the Jesus Prayer at a restaurant while he, half-listening, rambles on about the weekend ahead and eats his lunch of frog legs.

She is too taken up with her theme to eat and continues rather to explain that something happens when you say the prayer, some mystical effect. You just say the prayer over and over. It is not even necessary to believe, she tells him, quantity is more important than quality. It is like the Nembutsu sects of Buddhism saying Namu Amida Butsu, over and over again, and in the end you "see God" (pg. 37).

Eventually Franny's boyfriend becomes discomfited, somewhat peeved by her persistence, but then truly concerned for Fanny when she faints. Too late now for the football game, he leaves her to fetch a taxi to take her to her room. While he is gone, Franny, prone on the floor and quite still, is looking quietly at the ceiling when "her lips began to move, forming soundless words, and they continued to move" (Salinger, p. 44).

After the unfortunate weekend, Franny withdraws to the familiar childhood sur-roundings of her parent's New York apart-ment. Despondent, she arouses the concern of her Irish mother, the sympathy of her Jewish Father, and the sharp criticism of Zooey, her somewhat older brother. Zooey is familiar with the Jesus Prayer, as he explains to their mother, "It's nothing new... It didn't just start with the little pilgrim's crowd... In India, for God knows how many centuries, it's been known as 'japam'.... just the repetition of the names of God" (pg. 114).

Zooey tells his sister that if she were seri-ous about the Jesus Prayer she would not have come home to be babied but would have set out to find someone qualified to guide her in its use. Since she has come home, Zooey is determined to tell what he thinks, "qualified or not." He accuses her, in the first instance, of not knowing to whom she is praying. She is confusing Jesus, he tells her, with comfort-able images of St. Francis or "Heidi's grand-father." "Keep *him* in mind," he tells her, "and him only, and not as you'd like him to have been" (p. 169). "The Jesus Prayer," he explains, "has one aim… to endow the person who says it with Christ consciousness. Not to set up some little cozy, some holier than thou trysting place with some sticky, adorable, divine personage" (p. 172).

Zooey is critical of his sister, particularly in her negative attitude towards her teachers and others. He recommends detachment, desirelessness, and tells her that all the "others," even those she detests, are Christ Himself. He reminds her that as she came home, instead of looking for an experienced adviser, she is "only entitled to the low grade spiritual council" she might be able to find here. But in the end Franny seems content, appears to have acquired whatever wisdom she needed, goes to bed and falls "into a deep dreamless sleep… smiling at the ceiling." We never learn if she continues with the Jesus Prayer.

Though only a fictional account, Salinger's *Franny and Zooey* is a useful example of the Jesus Prayer employed out of the context of its tradition. Though less offensive, it is in a way comparable to Prime's 1850 view of Orthodoxy. He had no idea of the traditional significance or doctrinal framework which would have given meaning to the performance of the gorgeously-robed men he observed circling the table in the "Holy of holies." Zooey, as involuntary Starets, was apparently able to help his sister, but neither he nor Franny appear to understand the Jesus Prayer in the context of Orthodoxy.

V

OTHER SOURCES

When Salinger wrote *Franny and Zooey* in the mid-1950s, there were very few Orthodox sources available in English on the Jesus Prayer. Salinger might have been familiar with an English translation of the Russian *Writings from the Philokalia on Prayer of the Heart* which was published in London by Faber and Faber in 1951. But the first English edition of the Greek *Philokalia* did not begin to appear until 1979, while a third volume was published in 1984 followed by the final in 1995. These of course are older works, and are actually collections of still earlier ones.

To this category of ancient texts concerning the Jesus Prayer, recently made available in English, must be added *Triads* of Gregory Palamas, as edited by Father John Meyendorff, which appeared in 1983, and *The Ladder of Divine Ascent* by John Climacus with an extensive introduction by Bishop Kallistos Ware, which appeared in 1982.

A second category of translations includes more or less contemporary works. These include such books as Meyendorff's *A Study of Gregory Palamas*. Translated from the French, it first appeared in English in 1964. Also by the same author is *St. Gregory Palamas and Orthodox Spirituality*, which appeared in English in 1974. More general but also pertinent is Meyendorff's *The Orthodox Church* which appeared in English in 1981, and Father Alexander Schemann's *Historical Road of Eastern Orthodoxy*, translated from the Russian and published in this country in 1971. To these translated Orthodox sources must be added *The Name of Jesus* by the French scholar Irenee Hausherr, which appeared in English in 1978.

Other than Hausherr's book, which is a classic of sorts, and Steven Runciman's, *The Great Church in Captivity*, non-Orthodox works are not considered here. Assumed is that

Orthodox sources, though not always consistent with one another, see the Jesus Prayer
in the context of Orthodox tradition. With
so many recent translations of Orthodox
works into English, it is no longer necessary
to approach Orthodoxy indirectly. Fortunately,
for the direct approach, Oxford, which in the
1920s produced Robert Byron, in the post
World War II era produced Timothy Ware,
who went further than the Byzantine-ophiles
of the earlier period, became Orthodox, and
today, as Kallistos, titular Bishop of Diokleia,
is a recognized and prolific Orthodox author-
ity. The wheel has come full circle. Bishop
Kallistos's works on aspects of Orthodoxy
are now being translated into other languages.
Such is the case with his book, *The Power of
the Name, the Jesus Prayer in Orthodox Spirituality*,
which in 1982 appeared in Germany under the
title, *Hinführing zum Herzengebet*.

A contemporary Orthodox view of the Jesus
Prayer provides clues as to what to look for in
an historical search for the significance of the
Prayer through the centuries. Ware, because his
interpretation appears broader than others, is an
appropriate guide. For Ware, the Jesus Prayer,

"Lord Jesus Christ, Son of God, have mercy on me a sinner," has "marvelous versatility. It is a prayer for sinners, but equally a prayer that leads to the deepest mysteries of the contemplative life." (*The Orthodox Church*, pp. 312-313).

This twofold use by beginners and by the most advanced is a significant point that may help to explain misunderstanding about the Prayer. For Ware, "every Christian can use the prayer at odd moments." for example, "it can be used by anyone, at any time, in any place: standing in queues, walking, travelling on buses or trains; when at work; when unable to sleep at night; at times of special anxiety." Presumably Franny, had she tried this more casual beginner's approach, might have avoided a nervous breakdown.

"It is a different matter," Ware cautions, "to recite it more or less continually and to use the physical exercises which have become associated with it." For those who use the Prayer systematically, Ware reminds us, "Orthodox spiritual writers insist" that they "if possible, place themselves under the guidance of an experienced director and do nothing on their own initiative." For some of those who proceed in this way, "the Jesus Prayer enters the heart so that it is no longer recited by a deliberate effort, but recites itself spontaneously, continuing even when a man talks or writes, present in his dreams, waking him up in the morning." (Ibid). It is this second and systematic use of the prayer, combined with physical exercise, which suggests "Hesychasm," although this term, like the Jesus Prayer, appears to be applied by the Orthodox to different levels of spiritual activity.

As to the importance of the Jesus Prayer within the Orthodox tradition, Ware leaves no doubt. He says it is a personal prayer "which has for centuries played an extraordinarily important part in the life of the Orthodox." and is "surely the most classic of all Orthodox prayers." Authorities agree that it is ancient but are uncertain as to exactly how ancient.

VI

AN HISTORICAL SURVEY

In his book, *The Name of Jesus*, Irenee Hausherr provides an historical survey of the Jesus Prayer, which is a convenient point of departure for discussing what is known about its use and development over the centuries. Hausherr's thesis is that the earliest Hesychasts used a variety of short prayers in their meditations but that this freedom of practice gradually stabilized into a set prayer formula, the Jesus Prayer. It was a development which took nearly a millennium, and Hausherr, faced with a monkish and otherworldly lack of precision in dating many of the sources, tries nevertheless to pinpoint the highlights of the historical process.

He first defines precisely what it is he is tracing. The precise wording of the Jesus Prayer as given in the Philokalia and in *The Way of the Pilgrim*, he reminds us, is "Lord Jesus Christ, son of God, have mercy on me," with or without the addition of "a sinner." The prayer, he explains, has two elements, it is an appeal for mercy together with the name and title of the Savior, implying an act of faith in him as Messiah, as son of God, as God himself.

Hausherr's studies led him to conclude that the first historical evidence for the Jesus Prayer is to be found in the life of Saint Dosithy of Gaza. Dosithy was a novice, a young man with tuberculosis who cared for the sick. His spiritual father, the early Sixth Century Saint Dorotheos of Gaza, recommended the Jesus Prayer to him as the most appropriate for a young man still inexperienced in the life of the spirit. Dosithy's major struggle was against "self will," and he is remembered for his success in using the Jesus Prayer to overcome his selfishness. Typically, as befits a saint, he attributed his success to the prayers of his spiritual father Dorotheos.

In his youth, Dorotheos had been the disciple of two celebrated saints, Barsanuphius and John the Prophet, known from their letters to have recommended short prayers. From a number of prayers learned from these elders, Dorotheos selected the Jesus Prayer for young Dosithy, or so Hausherr believes. Hausherr's point being that at this time, the early fifth century, the Jesus Prayer was but one of a number of short prayers in use by the monks in Gaza. For the next step in the process whereby the Jesus Prayer becomes the preferred prayer, Hausherr turns to the account of a certain Abba Philemon about whom little is known.

Hausherr cannot be certain but favors the idea that Philemon lived in the early sixth century. (Hausherr, p. 273). What Hausherr finds as new in Philemon is the exclusive use of one formula: "Lord Jesus Christ (son of God), have mercy on me." (Hausherr, p. 275). The circumstances and reasons for Philemon's use of the prayer are also instructive.

Philemon emphasized continuous praying in the "heart." The heart, or "kardia" in Greek, is a concept closely associated with the Jesus Prayer in the Orthodox tradition. By "heart" the Orthodox do not mean simply the physical organ but the spiritual center of man's being, seat of the deepest and truest self, and all-embracing so as to include body, soul, and spirit (see *Philokalia I*, p. 361-362). Philemon wrote, "The heart that is pure becomes the dwelling place of the Holy Spirit and can see in all clarity, as in a mirror, the full reality of God" (Hausherr, p. 276).

As with Dorotheos, so with Philemon, the Jesus Prayer was an instrument for beginners. It was a remedy against a wandering imagination used to combat distractions and temptations, to purify the intellect of all thoughts but thoughts of God, and to make progress toward uninterrupted prayer (Hausherr, p. 275). The Jesus Prayer was not everything, but only part of a wider ascetic regimen including liturgical prayers.

From Philemon, possibly of the sixth century, Hausherr moves to a discussion of the Jesus Prayer in relation to the monks of Mount Sinai, whose spirituality came to them from Egypt and Palestine. His particular interest is in the Prayer as taught by the best known of the Sinai monks, John Climacus, who wrote toward the middle of the seventh century (Hausherr, p. 280). Saint Climacus makes only a few references to the Jesus Prayer but these were picked out and quoted over and over again by later Hesychasts.

Later Hesychasts, Hausherr implies, were not critical historians and read more into Climacus's references than the saint intended. A principal Jesus Prayer related text of Climacus is a reference to the uniting of the "memory of Jesus with your breathing" (Hausherr, p. 281). The phrase, Hausherr tells us, is older than Climacus, actually a more ancient tradition, meaning that one should remember Jesus whenever or as often as one breathes. Just how Saint Climacus intended this be accomplished is left somewhat open.

Hausherr, consistent with his thesis, emphasizes that John Climacus deliberately left the question of how to remember Jesus open. Each individual has different needs and different ways of accomplishing continued remembrance, Hausherr reminds us, and he quotes John Climacus to the effect that, "the bread of interior meditation is not necessarily the same for all" (Hausherr, p. 263).

Although the specific prayer formula may differ from individual to individual, John

Climacus is clear in recommending a short prayer, "Monologistos euche," as a prayer of one word. In this and in other respects his interpretation of Saint Climacus's views of the Jesus Prayer differ from that of Bishop Kallistos Ware.

Ware agrees that John recommended short simple prayers with various formulas but maintains that he attached particular importance to the Jesus Prayer. Hausherr, Ware believes, correctly warned against reading too much into John Climacus's "Name Of Jesus" references, but "surely goes too far in the opposite direction" (Ware, *Climacus*, p. 45). Because of John's great influence on later writers, Ware carefully examines each of his "Jesus Prayer" references.

Ware points out that John Climacus is the first author to have used the expression, "Jesus Prayer." He did so in his *Ladder of Divine Ascent*, while discussing thoughts presented to us by demons immediately before going to sleep. Along with the remembrance of death, "The concise Jesus Prayer," John recommends, should, "go to sleep with you and get up with you," for "nothing helps as these do when you are asleep" (*Climacus*, p. 46). Ware, disagreeing now with Hausherr, emphasizes that John did not here recommend just any short prayer, but the "concise Jesus Prayer." He concedes that probably at this time there were variations in the precise wording of the prayer, for the wording had not yet become stereotyped, but whatever the exact words, for John Climacus, the Jesus Prayer was a prayer of contrition and penitence linked with a remembrance of death and included, along with an invocation to Jesus, the words "have mercy on me," or the equivalent. The prayer was also a weapon against demons and was especially recommended for use when on the threshold of sleep.

Still another passage from *The Ladder*, the most important, Ware believes, relates the prayer to solitude or "stillness." It is the same passage noted by Hausherr for associating the remembrance of Jesus with breathing. The citation reads:

Stillness (hesychia) is worshipping God unceasingly and waiting on him. Let the remembrance of Jesus be present with your every breath. Then indeed you will appreciate the value of stillness (*The Ladder*, p. 48).

Although the Jesus Prayer is not specifically mentioned, Ware favors the thought that John Climacus meant the Jesus Prayer when using the phrase, "remembrance of Jesus," and this has been the way most later readers of *The Ladder* interpreted the passage. Assuming this to be the correct interpretation, there are a number of points of interest.

John Climacus intended that the remembrance of Jesus be as uninterrupted as possible, that it be present with every breath, or another translation, "united with your breath." Some see the passage as a metaphor, "remember God as often as you breathe." Others believe John had in mind a physical technique by which the Jesus Prayer is linked with the rhythm of breathing. Such a technique is advocated in early Coptic sources, but there are no unambiguous references to a breathing technique in the Greek tradition until the late thirteenth century (Ware in *The Ladder*, p. 49);

John Climacus's vague reference to breathing and the remembrance of Jesus was picked up and quoted by Hesychios, a monk of Sinai, and this gave it an added importance to later Hesychasts.

Hesychios of Sinai has been confused with Hesychius of Jerusalem who lived during the first half of the fifth century (see Rus Philokalia, p. 277). But today it is believed he was abbot of the Monastery of the Mother of God of the Burning Bush (Vatos) at Sinai. His dates are uncertain but he may belong to the eighth or even the ninth century. "He has a warm devotion to the Holy Name of Jesus," say the modern editors of *The Philokalia*, and his treatise "On Watchfulness and Holiness" is considered of "particular value to all who use the Jesus Prayer" (Philokalia I, p. 161). To Hausherr, Hesychios represents a further step in the history of the Jesus Prayer.

For Hausherr, Hesychios represents a halfway point between the complete freedom of individual monks to choose their own short prayer and the nearly exclusive use of the Jesus Prayer as we know it. But Hesychios made other contributions. Among other things, he was more poetic than many of the writers considered here. One citation shows this:

A heart that is utterly purged of fantasies will give birth to mysteries, divine ideas which will spring up in him like fish frolicking or dolphins dancing in a tranquil sea. As the water ripples with a light breeze, so does the Holy Spirit move in the depths of the heart, making us cry out, "Abba, Father."

To Hesychios the Jesus Prayer reformed many of the functions which John Climacus noted but there is a new element. The heart which for Climacus was defended from waywardness by the Jesus Prayer, now, according to Hesychios, also gains something, profitable thoughts, divine ideas. Physical asceticism associated with John Climacus remains, but with Hesychios asceticism is more pronouncedly interior and mental.

Hesychios also subscribed to the idea found in John Climacus of uniting remembrance of Jesus with breathing. He strengthened the metaphor, replacing "unite" with "cling," and elsewhere he wrote of "continual, uninterrupted breathing and calling on Christ Jesus" (Hausherr, p. 289). In later years these expressions would be taken literally, but Hausherr believes Hesychios used them only metaphorically.

Saint Dosithy and Saint Dorotheos of Gaza, Abba Philemon, Saint John Climacus, and Hesychios are the milestones by which Hausherr brings his history of the Jesus Prayer up to the year one thousand. He found nothing to indicate that up to that time the Jesus Prayer was the most popular prayer in the Byzantine monastic world. From that time until the thirteenth century there are few references to the Jesus Prayer. A well-documented exception is the Abba Isaiah who was spiritual director of Theodora, a nun, and the daughter of the Emperor Isaac II Angelus, who reigned twice between 1185 and 1204.

Abba Isaiah emphasized Hesychast spirituality to Theodora, and spoke to her of "secret meditation," by which he meant praying continually in the mind, "O Lord Jesus, have mercy on me. Son of God hear my prayer." Since a privileged person such as Theodora was not already familiar with the prayer, Hausherr concludes that the common faithful would be even less likely to have known it. The Jesus Prayer appears at this time to have been confined to monks and nuns, a form of "secret meditation" not widely known and practiced by lay people, as it seems to have been in mid-nineteenth century Russia of *The Way of the Pilgrim*.

In Russia, or rather the pre-Mongolian conquest Kiev-Rus, the Jesus Prayer appears to have been known by the beginning of the twelfth century. In 1106 Prince Nicholas Sviatosha became the first princely monk of Russia. He was known for never being idle either in the monastery's vegetable garden or making clothes. All the while he accompanied his work with unceasing recitation of the Jesus Prayer.

Nicholas was extremely active and for him and pre-Mongolian conquest Russia the Jesus Prayer was simply the shortest and easiest formula for perpetual praying. G. P. Fedotov, who tells of Nicholas in *The Russian Religious Mind*, emphasizes that there was little of the mystical strain in Kievan Christianity. Russia would wait another three centuries before its monks would adopt a more mystical use of the prayer. That development would follow a trend toward mysticism in the Greek centers of monasticism, a Hesychast revival, which began in the thirteenth century and is associated with Nicephorus the Hesychast (Fedotov, Vol. I, p. 388).

Before becoming a monk on Mount Athos, Nicephorus had been Italian, perhaps actually a Greek from Calabria or Sicily. A convert to Orthodoxy, he lived for a time in Constantinople during the reign of Emperor Michael VIII (1261-1282). He settled on Mount Athos where he first lived a cenobic life in common with other monks in obedience to a superior, but eventually he was permitted to become a Hesychast, or "solitary."

Nicephorus collected passages from the books and lives of the fathers with the purpose of demonstrating that there was a "method" or "science" by which one might ascend to communion with the Lord through prayer "of mind and heart." To each selection from the fathers he added brief comments to draw attention to a lesson being taught and related to his overall theme *On Vigilance and Custody of the Heart.* (Rus Philokalia, p.21, and Hausherr, p. 310).

Nicephorus made explicit a physical method, only suggested by such fathers as John Climacus, which was meant to facilitate entry into the heart by combining the Jesus Prayer with a breathing technique. His concern is for "custody of the heart," which has many names. It is sometimes called "custody of the mind," but also, "nepsis," and "vigilance." In any case it involves both mind (spiritual intellect) and heart, and Nicephorus often speaks of leading the mind into the heart. Or, more correctly, leading the wandering mind back into the heart. The mind (nous) or spiritual intellect (pneuma), as it is also called in the Orthodox tradition, is distinguished from reason. Unlike reason it does not function by formulating abstract concepts and arguing from them to a conclusion, but understands divine truth directly by intuition or "simple cognition." The spiritual intellect is sometimes called the innermost aspect of the "heart," (Philokalia I, p. 362) and in some contexts "heart and "intellect" are almost interchangeable (Ware, *The Orthodox Way*, p. 154).

Custody of the mind and heart, Nicephorus explains, involves constant watchfulness over one's inward thoughts and fantasies. The goal is apatheia, or "dispassion," perhaps best translated "purity of the heart" (Ware, *The Orthodox Way*, pg. 156). Nicephorus involves the body in the Hesychast efforts to achieve apathea, by recommending a posture and a way of breathing. This use of the body is consistent with the Orthodox view that man, unlike the angels, is a unity of body and soul. The body has its part to play, as in fasting, or prostrations during prayer, in achieving purity of heart (Ware, *The Orthodox Way*, p. 155).

It is not the bodily aspects of the Nicephorus method which interest Hausherr, but his use of the Jesus Prayer. It is significant for Hausherr's history of the prayer that it was an integral part of Nicephorus's psychophysical technique. His technique made the prayer the principal occupation of the mind. From his time Hausherr tells us the Jesus Prayer predominated in the Orthodox tradition over every other prayer formula. Even when other aspects of Nicephorus's method were downgraded, the Jesus Prayer "retained the place of supremacy" (Hausherr, p. 317).

Meyendorff agrees that the breathing method recommended by Nicephorus was directed toward those who for one reason or another had no access to a spiritual father or guidance and had to go it on their own. The breathing exercises were "a practical way to follow if one is deprived of an experienced master." Breathing exercises were secondary, but one of a number of ways of achieving purity, or "custody of the heart" (Meyendorff, pp. 56-63).

The Jesus Prayer has a more central role in Nicephorus teachings than breathing techniques. He writes, "If in spite of all your efforts (using the breathing technique) you do not succeed in entering the heart" there is another method which involves banishing all thoughts from the inner discourse which takes place in every man's breast (You can do this, he writes, if you want to) and replacing them with the prayer, "Lord, Jesus Christ, Son of God, have mercy upon me." The result of doing this with "strong desire and attention" is that a "whole host of virtues will come to you" (Rus Philokalia, pp. 33-34).

There is a difference of opinion as to the extent of Nicephorus's influence during his lifetime. When Gregory of Sinai (1255-1346) visited Mount Athos in the 1320s or thereabouts, he found only three monks who practiced contemplation, mental prayer, and guarding of the mind in the manner taught by Nicephorus (Philokalia, Russ, p. 35). Gregory was from Asia Minor, had spent some years at the monastery at Sinai, which explains his surname, but appears to have learned of custody of the mind and pure prayer from a monk named Arsenius on the island of Crete, where he later lived. Gregory made full use of the experience of earlier generations, combining concepts from the Divine Ladder of John Climacus, presumably learned at Sinai, with the spiritual doctrine of pure prayer. His writings are still popular among Orthodox monks.

Gregory was forced to flee Athos in 1325 because of recurring attacks by the Turks, but eventually settled in the mountains of Thrace, at the boundary of the Byzantine Empire and Bulgaria. From there his influence and Hesychasm spread into the Slavic countries. Bulgarian disciples of Gregory of Sinai passed the Hesychast method on to intermediaries like Cyrian, the metropolitan of Kiev (1376-1406), and in this way Hesychasm reached Russia in the fourteenth century (Meyendorff,

An Historical Survey

St. Gregory Palamas and Orthodox Spirituality, pp. 63-64; and Robert L. Nichols, "The Orthodox Elders (Startsy) of Imperial Russia," *Modern Greek Studies Yearbook*, Vol. 1, 1985, p. 5).

Nicephorus and Gregory of Sinai each made a contribution to the spread of Hesychasm within the monastic communities of the Byzantine Empire and beyond. But neither was a theologian and equipped if necessary to defend the Hesychast method from outside criticism. The task of integrating Hesychasm into Orthodox theology by setting it on a firm dogmatic base fell to a contemporary of St. Gregory of Sinai, Gregory Palamas.

Palamas was also a monk on Mount Athos where he had been introduced to Hesychasm during long years under the direction of a spiritual father. Like Gregory of Sinai, he also left the Holy Mountain around 1325 because of Turkish intrusion. But Gregory Palamas's background was exceptional in a way that set him aside from the more simple monks.

Palamas was born in 1296 in Constantinople of a noble family close to the imperial court of Emperor Andronicus II. He lost his father as a boy but was educated at imperial expense for a secular career and with a curriculum based on classical philosophy. This formal training, particularly in the *Logics* of Aristotle, was to be of use when, in the 1330s, he was called on to defend Hesychasm and the manner of prayer which since Nicephorus had become associated with it (Meyendorff, *Triads*, p. 5).

Palamas's opponent was Barlaam the Calabrian, also called the Philosopher. He arrived in Constantinople from Italy in the 1330s and was soon well known as a scholar. A contemporary of the Italian humanist Petrarch (1304-1374), Barlaam grew up in an Italy already stirring with the spirit of the Renaissance and seeking to free itself from the Middle Ages and the Thomist school of philosophy. He was inclined toward innovation in theology, and had an inquiring mind.

When, for example, Barlaam clashed with the monks of Constantinople, he determined to find out more about them and for a while shared the life of the Hesychast hermitages at Constantinople and Thessalonica. There he was introduced to the psychophysical method of prayer along lines prescribed by Nicephorus and other Hesychasts. He was profoundly shocked (Meyendorff, *St. Gregory Palamas and Orthodox Spirituality*, pg. 89).

Not only were the monks Barlaam met poorly educated, but they professed to know of things he refused to believe. Particularly abhorrent to him was their "materialism" expressed in their insistence that the human body could participate in prayer and benefit from divine grace. Equally offensive, they insisted that through the practice of Hesychasm it was possible to experience a vision of Divine, Uncreated Light, the same Light which the three disciples saw surrounding Jesus at his Transformation at Mount Tabor (Ware, *The Orthodox Church*, pg. 75).

Indignant, Barlaam, in Constantinople in 1338, circulated attacks on the monks and eventually officially complained about them to the Patriarch, John Calecas, who dismissed the complaint and advised Barlaam to leave the monks in peace (Meyendorff, *A Study of Gregory Palamas*, pg. 46). Ignoring the advice of the Patriarch, Barlaam continued to attack the monks. Finally, in 1341 at Thessalonica, Gregory Palamas wrote the first of his *Triads* in defense of the Hesychasts.

Barlaam's criticism of Hesychast practices had affected more than the lives of the monks, as it touched on doctrinal questions of fundamental importance to Orthodoxy, such as how man can know a transcendent God and the role of the body in the life of the spirit. These and other profound questions related to Hesychasm and use of the Jesus Prayer Palamas now answered systematically and in ways that involved the entire Orthodox tradition.

The narrow trail which we have been following in pursuit of the historical significance of the Jesus Prayer now, in the fourteenth century, widens for a time to include the vast landscape of all late Byzantine Christianity and its way of looking at the world, as opposed to a newer way on which the West was about to embark. Of the subtly divergent ways of seeing man and his relationship to God, one way was eventually to dominate the Christian West, and the other the Christian East.

VII

BARLAAM VS. PALAMAS

Barlaam's position in the Hesychast quarrel was based on two assumptions. One, Aristotelian, assumed all knowledge, including knowledge of God, to be derived from sensory experience. The other neoplatonic, but also based on Christian writers, maintained that God is beyond sensory experience and therefore unknowable. Further, Barlaam viewed man in the Platonic sense, as soul imprisoned in a body. Palamas, while he recognized a certain value in ancient philosophy, could not accept Barlaam's way of thinking, which denied all possibility of direct intervention of the Spirit in man's knowledge of God. Further, Palamas rejected Plato's view of the soul's imprisonment in the body.

In contrast to the Platonic view, he argued for the dignity of matter and the Biblical concept in which sacramental grace sanctifies the whole man and pledges bodily resurrection on the last day.

For Palamas, from the time when the Son of God took flesh in the womb of Mary, the supernatural could no longer be regarded as immaterial. In Meyendorff's words, "Since the Incarnation, our bodies have become temples of the Holy Spirit who dwells in us." The Hesychasts were right when they sought the Holy Spirit within their own bodies because within our bodies, "sanctified by the sacraments and engrafted by the Eucharist into the Body of Christ," God is to be found. The light of Mount Tabor which Peter, James, and John saw externally in the story of the Transfiguration, and which was a foretaste of the second coming, is now to be found within the heart. The special goal of the monks was to contemplate this light, and develop its potentialities until they found God himself (Meyendorff, *St. Gregory Palamas and Orthodox Spirituality*, pp. 108-118).

VIII

HESYCHASM AS SELF

INDULGENCE

In his account of Palamas's contribution, Meyendorff also addresses another aspect of Hesychasm and the Jesus Prayer, i.e. whether or not preoccupation with such matters is not, after all, individualistic and self indulgent. It has been so considered, even by Orthodox spokesmen. The Reverend Nicon D. Patrinacos, in his book, *All that a Greek Orthodox Should Know*, views Hesychasm as an unfortunate aspect of declining Byzantium. It was the "coup de grace," he writes, "for genuine Patristic theology in the Orthodox Church and the beginning of a spirituality deriving from the individual as against the collective and balanced spiritual life of the church" (p. 69). Significantly, in a companion volume, *A Dictionary of Greek Orthodoxy*, Patrinacos does not even mention the Jesus Prayer, although Prayer as such is treated extensively.

Patrinaco's view may represent an alternative Orthodox tradition associated in his case with a political form of Hellenism of which merges Greek Orthodox and Greek nationalist sentiments. For him, Hesychasm is of little value either to the collective of the Church or of the State. Indeed it does appear that while Palamas's defense of Hesychasm assumes its practice within a doctrinal and liturgical environment, for Hesychasts like St. Gregory of Sinai participation in the liturgy was less important, perhaps even harmful. Other spokesmen for Orthodoxy see matters differently.

For Meyendorff the "true nature" of Hesychast spirituality is demonstrated in the lives of two late thirteenth century personalities, both of whom recommended the Jesus Prayer and Hesychast methods, Patriarch Athanasius I, and a pupil of Nicephorus,

Theoleptus, Metropolitan of Philadelphia. Neither, Meyendorff tells us, was a hermit shut up in a cloister or hidden in the desert. Both are associated with social and spiritual reform and sought to encourage ecclesial community and the sacramental spirit in Byzantium. They show, Meyendorff insists, that "fourteenth century Hesychasm was not an individualistic mystical movement, but a spiritual renewal based on patristic tradition" (Meyendorff, p. 63).

Church councils of June and August 1341, held in the galleries of Santa Sophia in Constantinople, vindicated Gregory Palamas and condemned Barlaam. The Calabrian Philosopher returned to Italy, eventually became a bishop there, and in his old age taught Greek, with indifferent success, to Petrarch. Gregory Palamas was to experience five years of political harassment and be charged with heresy between 1343 and 1347, but in May of the latter year he was consecrated archbishop of Thessalonica. Gregory died in 1359 and was named a saint shortly afterwards. His life was still another example, Meyendorff reminds us, of a Hesychast who, when he was called to do so, left his monastic retreat and plunged into dogmatic controversy and the social and political life of his time.

IX

THE END OF THE EMPIRE

In May of 1453, less than a century after the death of Palamas, the Byzantine Empire was no more. Constantinople fell to the Turks to complete the gradual conquest which had already been going on during Palamas's life. An episode with the Turks involving Saint Gregory displays a surprising aspect of Christian-Muslim relations and helps to explain how under Turkish rule Byzantine monasticism and spirituality was able to survive.

Toward the end of his life, Archbishop Gregory was making a voyage from Thessalonica to Constantinople when the vessel on which he was traveling was captured by the Turks. He and the other passengers were forced to spend a year in captivity in Asia Minor, already under Turkish control. Gregory's letters from this period show a tolerant attitude of Turks toward Christians. Gregory carried on amicable debates with the son of his captor on religious questions and expressed the hope that the "day would soon come when we will be able to understand one another" (Meyendorff, *St. Gregory Palamas and Orthodox Spirituality*, pg. 106).

Doubtless progress toward the understanding for which Gregory hoped has been slow, but regret for the fall of the Empire, and justifiable outrage at certain aspects of Turkish rule, can not obscure the fact that between 1453 and the establishment of Modern Greece in the nineteenth century, Orthodoxy, and consequently Hesychasm and the Jesus Prayer, survived in the Turkish Empire. On Mount Athos in particular monasticism continued much as before. Hesychasm, the quest in stillness for the God within, would seem to have been an admirably suited avenue for expression of spirituality for persons or whole peoples deprived of more openly demonstrative means.

X

THE JESUS PRAYER IN RUSSIA

But before returning to Hesychasm and the Jesus Prayer in Turkish-ruled areas of the former Byzantine Empire, their arrival and influence in another Orthodox area, Russia, must be noted. Throughout the years during which the Byzantine Empire was falling bit by bit to the Turks, what was to become Russia was freeing itself from a century long domination by another Muslim people, the Mongols. By 1453 this process had been all but completed. Moscow and its rulers had emerged as the dominant power in Russian lands.

As we have seen, the Jesus Prayer was known and practiced in pre-Mongol Kiev-Rus by such monks as Nicholas Svjatosha, but the students of the religious life and mind of the period such as Fedotov find no association of the prayer with anything that might be identified as mysticism. In the fourteenth century Hesychasm arrived in Russia from Bulgaria. St. Sergius of Radonezh, who died in 1392 after founding the Holy Trinity Lavra, is known to have practiced the Jesus Prayer and to have lived for a time as a hermit. In the following century, Saint Nilus Sorski (1433-1508) devoted his life to Hesychast spirituality (Nichols, *The Orthodox Elders of Imperial Russia*, pg. 3).

Saint Nilus visited Mount Athos and Constantinople in his youth and was befriended by the starets Paisius Yaroslavov, who may have been Nilus's spiritual father. Nilus believed monks should live lives of utter simplicity, without wealth or property, and he carried out this idea when he founded a skete in an isolated forest in the Russian North near the river Sora. Because of Nilus's position on monastic poverty, his party was known as the "non-possessors." He was welcomed by Ivan the Great, who gladly acquired monastic property so as to raise funds for his many building projects and to be able to give land to his supporters, the Dvorianstovo.

Nilus's ascetic rule of poverty was not an end in itself, but as he told in his writings on the spiritual life, the first Russian summary of the ascetic doctrine of the ancient fathers, the goal was "mental prayer," the method of the Hesychasts. He recommended the Jesus Prayer, in full or in abbreviated form. "In the beginning," he wrote, one must "make his heart silent and free from every cogitation." There is no room for visions of any kind, even of the celestial world, but the novice looks continually into the depth of the heart and says, "Lord Jesus Christ, Son of God, have mercy upon me." This one does insistently, "either standing or sitting or lying, closing your mind and heart and restraining your breath, breathing as slowly as possible" (Fedotov, Vol. II, p. 281-282).

Nilus held that the mental prayer was fitting for everyone, but recognized that it was sadly impossible to dwell always at the heights of prayer. There must be time, he said, to work for our brethren. Alms for the poor and hospitality to strangers, on the other hand, was limited by the poverty of the community. In this respect Nilus's views of Hesychast responsibilities toward the spiritual life as opposed to obligations beyond the immediate community may be said to be closer to those of St. Gregory of Sinai than to Saint Gregory Palamas, and they differed greatly from those of his contemporary Joseph of Volok.

Also a monastic leader, Joseph of Volok (1439-1515) believed that monasteries required both money and property, to purchase icons, books, and vestments and to feed not only the brethren but passers by and wanderers and to give alms to the poor. Joseph emphasized external order and liturgical prayer. The way to the internal for Joseph was through the external. "First," he wrote, "let us attend to bodily decency and orderliness and after that to the inner observance." Despite his undisputed holiness, Joseph was a practical business man, while Nilus recommended that his brothers, in the interest of their spiritual well being, carry out unavoidable business transactions in such a way that they worked to their own disadvantage.

The opposing views of Nilus and Joseph were to reverberate throughout the history of the Russian Church. The contemplative life of the Hesychast, which emphasized inner spirituality, was to experience a revival in eighteenth century Russia. It was a revival related to the religious policies of the Tsars of Russia, but also to the publication in 1782 of a collection of patristic texts on prayer, *The Philokalia*, and put together by St. Nicodemus the Hagiorite, (1748-1809), an Athonite monk, with the help of St. Makarios of Corinth (1731-1805).

The Philokalia, which Bishop Ware calls "an encyclopedia of Athonite learning," (p. 110) and which is given its "inner unity," in the words of its recent translation, by its "recurrent references to the Jesus Prayer," (*Philokalia I*, p.15) is evidence of the continuity of the Hesychast tradition during the years of Turkish dominions over the lands of the former Byzantine Empire. A gigantic book of 1207 folio pages when printed in Venice in 1782, *The Philokalia* dealt chiefly with the theory and practice of prayer, especially the Jesus Prayer (Ware, p. 110).

Nicodemus's collection of works from authors living in the fourth to the fifteenth century, some of them otherwise lost, became one of the most influential books in Orthodox history. Though he valued Hesychasm and the Jesus Prayer, Nicodemus and those around him, Bishop Ware tells us, also attached much importance to the sacraments and advocated frequent communion, an unusual position for his time (Ware, pg. 110).

In 1793, less than a dozen years after the original Greek edition of *The Philokalia* was published in Venice, a Slavo-Russian translation was published in St. Petersburg. The translation was the work of the Ukrainian monk Paisii Velichkovsky (1722-1794). The Slavo-Russian translation of *The Philokalia* appeared at a critical moment for Russian monasticism. Catherine the Great (1762-1796) began her reign with a confiscation of monastic lands. She closed many monasteries and imprisoned those who protested. Her aim, apart from enriching the treasury of the state at the expense of the church, appears to have been an "enlightened" church more in tune with Western European developments (Nichols, p.7).

In her efforts to change the Russian Church, Catherine gave her support to three prominent personalities, the Metropolitan of St. Petersburg, Gavriil Petrov (1730-1801); the Metropolitan of Moscow, Platon Levshin (1749-1812); and the

Bishop of Voronezh, Tikhon Sokolov (1724-1783). At one time or another in their lives all three of these Orthodox churchmen appear to have been influenced by pietistic and sentimental ideas originating in Western Europe.

Pietism emphasized the priesthood of all believers, regarded religion as more an affair of the heart than the intellect, and was philanthropic in orientation. It was also individualistic. A second western European influence was the sentimentalism of Rousseau which combined religious temperament and a love for the solitary life with a desire to cultivate kindness, generosity, honesty, and sympathetic understanding for others. Influenced to varied degrees by these western ideas, Gavriil, Platon, and Tikhon were nonetheless firmly rooted in their own Orthodox tradition, in particular that represented by *The Philokalia*. The result was a particularly Russian development which brought Russian monasticism in touch with the broader strata of Russian society and popularized aspects of Hesychasm, including the Jesus Prayer.

Gavriil, who supervised editing of the Slavo-Russian translation of the Philokalia prepared by Paisii, contributed to the revival of Russian monasticism and the emergence of the Russian *startsy* by encouraging the establishment of hermitages as training grounds for these spiritual elders. Platon had a similar career. He was responsible for rebuilding the Optina hermitage near Kozelsk, a small town in central Russia. Optina was to become the most famous of all the startsy cloisters. It is the life, however, of St. Tikhon of Zadonsk that blends the new Western influences with a solidly grounded Orthodoxy.

Unlike Gavriil and Platon, Tikhon chose to give up his role as a high church official. In 1768 he received Catherine's permission to retire to the monastery at Zadonsk. His life is characterized by a blending of the contemplative way with charity toward others. Familiar with elements of the Western mystical tradition as well as patristics, he practiced the Jesus Prayer while emphasizing charity toward others and showing concern for the spiritual life of ordinary Russians. He also revived the non-possessor stance of St. Nilus of Sora.

In freeing the church of possessions, something in which Catherine could also take pleasure, Tikhon was partly bowing to necessity, but he was also bringing the church closer to the people of Russia. Tikhon strengthened these ties by emphasizing service to the poor, the sick, the orphaned, and the widowed. "What was remarkable," writes Robert L. Nichols, "was the direct approach to religious life which allowed for personal experimentation and a new freedom" (Nichols, p. 10).

In response to Nichols, it can be argued that a direct approach to religious life and freedom was integral to the Hesychast tradition and neither remarkable nor new. What was new perhaps were the Russian conditions which led to the popularizing of the tradition so that elements of Hesychasm, the Jesus Prayer in particular, were no longer practiced only by monks but became the property of the common people as well.

To compliment the popularity of the direct approach to religious life, Russia produced, during the reign of Alexander I, a folk hero in the person of St. Seraphim of Sarov (1759-1833). Seraphim was "truly the guardian angel of his people" in the words of his biographer Valentine Zander (quoted by Nichols, p. 10).

As a young man he studied at the monastery at Sarov. There he became familiar with *The Philokalia* and other ascetical writings. When, in 1795, Seraphim withdrew to the wilderness to live like a hermit, he practiced the Jesus Prayer and contemplated "the invisible" in a life of silence and isolation. Only after 1810 when he left the wilderness and entered the Sarov cloister did he become regularly available to visitors, who sometimes counted in the thousands in a single day. To the novices that approached him he counseled, "learn to be peaceful and thousands of souls around you will find salvation" (Nichols, p.11).

According to one tradition, the Tsar Alexander abandoned his throne in 1825 and lived thereafter as a starets on the advice of Seraphim. Whether truth or legend, the story attests to the influence popularly attributed to the saint.

Seraphim was but one of a number of well known early nineteenth century starets. A center for these spiritual elders developed around the newly established (in 1821) skete of St. John the Baptist, a retreat not far from the Optina hermitage. Many of the skete's members were disciples of Paisii or were former members of Paisii's monastery in Moldavia.

Among them, arch monk Leonid Nagolkin (1768-1841) practiced the Jesus Prayer and became very accomplished. He could, he said, continue inward prayer without interruption while carrying on lengthy conversations out of love for one of his neighbors. Indeed, it was a talent for which he had frequent use. Church authorities became concerned when hundreds of visitors streamed to the contemplative cell for guidance. Forbidden by his superior to receive visitors, he rebelled and continued to give out spiritual guidance to those who sought him out.

Nichols finds something new, bold, and innovative in the way the *startsy* talked with lay people, and in the advice they gave. Others disagree and emphasize the words of the *startsy* Makarii (1788-1860) who said, "I have told you nothing that is an invention of my own. All of what I say comes from the writings of the fathers" (quoted by Nichols, p.14). Whether or not the *startsy* were original in the content of their guidance, they undeniably pushed "the diffusion of an essentially monastic spirituality into lay and secular circles" (quoted by Nichols, p. 13).

Starets Makarii died in 1860, about the time of the events described in *The Way of the Pilgrim*. To that extent this narrative has come full circle and many of the questions raised by Franny and Zooey would seem to have been answered. Still, since Salinger published his popular novel, Orthodox writers have begun to react to an expanding Western and non-Orthodox interest in the Jesus Prayer.

XI

ORTHODOX REACTION

Between the extremes of the prominent French Jesuit and scholar, Father Hausherr, and the American novelist Salinger, a great many Western lay and clerical persons have recently shown interest in Eastern spirituality and the Jesus Prayer. This was particularly true in the 1960s. What, one might ask, do the Orthodox think about this lately discovered curiosity? A source not yet conveniently available in English, *Tradition and Freedom in Orthodox Spirituality* by the Rumanian Metropolitan of Ardeal, Dr. Antonie Plamadeala, tells of the author's experiences while studying and traveling in the West in the 1960s.

Metropolitan Antonie traveled in the West as a simple monk from Northern Moldavia. His book, meant for Rumanian and Orthodox eyes, presents the author's impressions of Western spirituality, but this is incidental, a pretext, he writes in his introduction, to say more about Orthodoxy.

Metropolitan Antonie was impressed with the knowledge of Orthodox spirituality and theology which he found in the "well informed Westerner" of the 1960s. "He has heard of the Jesus Prayer and, from one end to the other tries to practice it," comments Antonie, then continues, "he has translated his Philokalia and Paterrikon, he knows St. Gregory Palamas, St. Maximus the Confessor and St. Simeon the New Theologian better than Easterners…" All these, he writes, the well-informed Westerner treats as hidden treasures which have been ignored until now.

In brief, the Westerner is derailed because he finds it difficult to live with the paradoxes of Orthodox thinking. "He doesn't understand exactly what is escaping him, why he too can't be at rest and satisfied between plus and minus as we are." The Orthodox respond to the

Westerner's questions about special "states" by saying they are and they aren't important, that they can and cannot be realized, and that they interest the Orthodox and they don't. The Eastern Orthodox see no difficulty in contradiction, Antonie explains, when they appear in "harmonious synthesis."

Consistent with his explanation of Orthodox thinking, Antonie responds to the Westerner's expectation that the Orthodox have access to "exceptional states" with the paradoxical explanation that "in everyday Orthodoxy the exceptional is the absence of the exceptional. Of course there are Hesychasts," he tells us, "we still have a few today." Then he quotes St. Varsanufie of the Sixth Century who claimed there weren't in his time more than three perfect people on earth.

Antonie summarizes the Western view as he experienced it: "The mistake of those who know Orthodoxy late and from outside is that they reduce it to its highest, most difficult, and most inaccessible-- to Hesychasm. They see all Orthodox as some permanent reciters of the Jesus Prayer, as contemplatives; they believe

that all of us are Hesychasts. Without doubt
Westerners know more about Hesychasm than
we Eastern Orthodox do. We don't talk much
about it" (p. 25).

Antonie does, nevertheless, have some
things to say about the Jesus Prayer. He does
so in the context of the overall theme of his
book "tradition and freedom." This theme
was suggested to him in the West during the
1960s. There, especially in the monastic life
he observed, he found the lack of freedom
which comes from subordination to a rule. He
recommended two things, apparently contra-
dictory. "Putting the accent back on tradition
and liberation from tradition." The tradition
to be accented was the authentic tradition of
experience lived and verified down through the
ages. The tradition from which one must be
liberated was the tradition which had become
"a dead letter, a form, a formalism, a Rule for
itself, a mechanism, inertia."

The implications here for the Jesus Prayer
are easily arrived at. The West tends to look to
the Jesus Prayer as a substitute for a rule, as a
mechanism. In the West Antonie was asked to
make a short presentation on the Jesus Prayer

and demonstrate its use. He replied that the initiation would take a lifetime. It is no "technique" he told his audience. Where technique is involved, "we are no longer speaking of Hesychasm."

There is no particular way in which the Jesus Prayer must be carried out, Antonie explains. Tradition provides for it being said while seated with the head between the knees, while walking, even in bed before going to sleep. Authentic tradition permits freedom here as in other Orthodox matters. Also there is no guarantee of results, no assurance that any special state will ever be achieved. This measure of uncertainty is another aspect of learning to live as the Eastern Orthodox do, "between plus and minus."

Perhaps it is because they represent "Western" Eastern Orthodoxy, there was no talk of living "between plus and minus" when, in March 1977, the three translators and editors of the English language edition of the Greek *Philokalia*, G. E. H. Palmer, Philip Sherrard, and Kallistos Ware, jointly signed the introduction to the first volume of their joint effort. Aware, no doubt, of some possible confusion in minds of their English speaking readers as to the role of the Jesus Prayer in the Orthodox tradition, they provide guidance which, here at least, must serve as the last word on the subject.

The editors stress that Hesychasm cannot be followed in a vacuum and that texts in *The Philokalia*, though seldom specifically doctrinal, "all presuppose doctrine." They remind us that living texts in *The Philokalia* were written by and for people living within the sacramental and liturgical life, not only of the Church, but under the special conditions of monasticism. Nevertheless, unceasing prayer is not something reserved for monks alone, they say. The spiritual path is open to all, they tell us, "provided that the basic conditions of active participation in the sacramental and liturgical life of the Church are fulfilled." They do, however, recommend personal guidance from a qualified teacher (p.16).